Be Inspired by
M.K.O. ABIOLA

Always Shine xxx
oro
Feb 2024

Written by
Olamidotun Votu-Obada

Illustrated by
Adedotun Akande

Copyright© 2022 by Inspire HQ

All rights reserved. No portion of this book may be reproduced – mechanically, transmitted or by any other means including photocopying, recording, or otherwise – without written permission of the author and publisher.

Published in Canada.

Library Cataloging-in-Publication Data is available

Be Inspired by MKO
Book : ISBN 978-1-7782222-4-5

For more information on the author -
www.olamidotunvo.com

For more works of the illustrator -
www.linktr.ee/collectiblecomicsng

First Edition - Published in July 2022

Inspire HQ

www.myinspirebooks.com

DEDICATION

This book is dedicated to every inspiring African leader that is genuinely striving for change in African countries across the world.

All dreams are possible. Change starts with us.

Keep going, keep shining, keep moving.

— OVO

DISCLAIMER

To tell the story of this inspiring and historic character, we have researched and written based on facts, history, and available information. Some parts that are unfortunately unverifiable. Some parts of this book have also been written as fiction, speculations to make it relatable to the reader.

No part of this book may be quoted as exact events. Some parts of this book are according to newspaper articles and articles online that are not verifiable. Hence, readers should beware not to take the contents of this book as factual evidence of the exact events that happened in the character's life.

The entire point of this story is to inspire and retell the story of this inspiring character as much as possible to the reader.

To the reader, read on and be inspired.

Inspire HQ Team

CONTENTS

Chapter I – Early Life

Chapter II – Moshood Kashimawo Olawale Abiola

Chapter III – Glasgow, Scotland

Chapter IV – Thinking Big

Chapter V – Politics

Chapter VI – The Presidential Election

Chapter VII – The Annulment

Chapter VIII – Legacy of an Icon

Chapter 1 — Early Life

Birth

On August 24th, 1937, Salawu Abiola held his newborn son. He wanted to feel love for the boy, but had already witnessed 22 of his other children die shortly after birth, so it was difficult. The Yoruba cocoa tradesman had no reason to think the boy would survive.

At the time, no one in Nigeria knew of the disease that had killed them — so they were simply known as those "born to die." In the Yoruba language, they were called "Abiku." Local folklore stated that the children only came to the world for a moment and could not wait to go back.

Right away, they named the boy "Kashimawo." It was a typical name given to Abiku children in an attempt to keep them in this world. The name meant "let's wait and see if he remains."

Five days later, when the boy had beaten all odds, they still found it hard to believe he would live much longer.

"What do you want to name him?" Salawu Abiola's wife, Suliat (also often referred to as Zeliat), asked her husband.

Salawu knew his son deserved a real name but he could not bring himself to give him one. His heart had been broken too many times. He stood up from the table and said, "Kashimawo."

Suliat (Zeliat) gave him an awkward look as he walked out of the room.

She was not pleased.

"One day," she whispered to her little boy, "You will have a real name and the world will know who you are."

2

Risk and Reward

Kashimawo's parents were very hard-working traders. His father traded in Cocoa while his mother traded in Kola Nuts. These two products were very high-risk and rewarding, meaning they could make the family a lot of money, but also carried a high risk of losing everything!
The boy helped his father — mostly after school — until his father's cocoa business suddenly collapsed!
One day, his father prepared a big shipment of cocoa. It was ready to be sent out. But then, it was flagged by a produce inspector as too low in quality.
"What?" Salawu questioned the inspector. "How is this shipment low in quality?"
The inspector did not explain his decision. He ruled that it could not be exported and ordered it be seized by the authorities. He promised that it would be destroyed.
The family had lost a lot of money and it ended Salawu's business for a while.

Firewood

Thankfully, his parents' good business sense and hard work had rubbed off on the young boy. The business failure did not discourage him. Instead, it motivated him to start making his own money. At the age of 9, Kashimawo started selling firewood.

This was when the poor people of the area still used firewood and charcoal to cook food. Only the rich could afford to use kerosene or electric stoves!

Kashimawo created a routine for himself. He woke up early at dawn, walked to a nearby forest, and picked dry sturdy branches. These branches were the firewood he would sell once he got out of school that day. He knew his family needed help, so he used the money he made to assist in feeding everyone.

Eventually, Kashimawo graduated from primary school and began to attend a high school for boys in Abeokuta, in the western part of Nigeria.

Chapter 11 — Moshood Kashimawo Olawale Abiola

Musician

At the age of 15, Kashimawo was finally given a proper name. Truth be told, everyone already knew him as Kashimawo, but it still felt great to be properly named!

"Moshood Kashimawo Olawale Abiola." He remembered his father uttering those words for the rest of his life. It was a great memory for the man who would become known as MKO; or Abiola, if that's what you prefer.

Then, MKO got another idea: He would start a musical band! The band played at different parties and ceremonies, which at first did not pay them any money; all they got was some food in return for performing. As they became more known, they requested money to perform, and MKO found himself with enough funds to support his family and pay for his education at high school.

Things were beginning to look good!

6

Ingenuity and Success

The high school for boys he attended in Abeokuta had an in-house magazine, The Trumpeter. MKO quickly became its editor.

His deputy at the magazine, Olusegun Obasanjo, was also destined to make history; he became the President of Nigeria many decades later. MKO and Obasanjo worked well together. Their friendship extended well beyond their high school years.

At the age of 19, he joined the National Council of Nigeria and the Cameroons, one of the first political parties in Nigeria. Abiola preferred the centrist NCNC over the left-leaning Action Group political party, led by Chief Obafemi Awolowo.

He also started working for Barclays Bank, which was one of the few banks operating in Nigeria at the time. The bank was located over 70 miles away in a big town called Ibadan; very far from home!

Love

While still in high school, Abiola met the love of his life, Simbiat, at the Arabic Quranic School in Abeokuta. She was born into one of the most prominent families in the city; the Soaga family.

Simbi — as her friends called her — was one year younger than Abiola, but they fell deeply in love with one another. Her family was not thrilled with their daughter's interest in the poor boy, but she felt her love for Abiola was genuine.

Her entire family argued that he had no chance of succeeding in life because he came from such a poor family. "Simbiat," her mother pleaded. "You have everything. Do not throw it all away!" "He is beneath you, daughter," Mr. Soaga added.

"Not everything is about status, dad!" Simbi could not believe she was having this conversation again. "How will he support you?" He asked for what seemed like the twentieth time. "Why can't you understand?" Simbi was in tears. This conversation was going nowhere. MKO knew they disapproved and, after some time, he grew tired because he knew they were correct. He did come from a poor home and he could not fight back. Simbi would not give up and told her family that he was the one for her. She was adamant that nothing would change her mind! Due to her wealthy lifestyle, Simbi was able to show Abiola a new side of life; one he had never seen before. For instance, the young Abiola got to try eggs for the first time! Eggs were reserved for only the wealthiest Nigerians (and for older people). He thought they were amazing! Their love blossomed and the young couple were soon married in a traditional Yoruba wedding.

Chapter III — Glasgow, Scotland

Higher Education

In 1960, MKO went to university. He had received a scholarship from the government of Nigeria to attend the University of Glasgow in Scotland, where he would study accounting.

His wife joined him in Scotland a year later.
Their reunion at the airport in Scotland was touching. They had not seen each other for months. Simbi held her husband for what seemed like minutes! It was so good to be back together again!
"I'm going to enroll in school," she told him.
Abiola nodded knowingly. "I know."
"How do you know?" She was taken aback by his certainty.
"Simbi, your family is full of great female high-achievers," he smiled at her. "Why would my wife be any different?
I know you're the studious type!"
Simbi enrolled at the Robroyston Hospital in Glasgow to study Nursing and eventually graduated in Arts & Fashion Design from the Rodimus College of Art. She also got certified in Interior Decoration by the School of Domestic Science in Glasgow; high-achiever, indeed!

Marriage

Their Yoruba wedding was not officially legal, so the couple got married again in Glasgow on the 2nd day of October, 1960. The exact place was the Registration District of Kelvin in Glasgow. This made their wedding legal.

They celebrated with a nice stroll through a park in Glasgow on that chilly night. "What should we do after we graduate, my love?" Simbi asked, holding on to Abiola's arm for warmth. They had a few choices; remain in Scotland and earn a living, go back to Nigeria, or maybe even head to the United States!

"How would you feel about staying here for a while?" Abiola suggested. "Well, let's see," Simbi said. "Nigeria is warm. It is our homeland. We are comfortable there. Scotland is beautiful... but it's also cold, it rains all the time, and you'll never get me to try Haggis."

"You don't have to try Haggis," he reassured her. "Then," she answered in a chipper voice. "Let's stay!" Their laughter echoed throughout the freezing-cold park.

Work and Family

Upon graduation from the *University of Glasgow*, Abiola was employed as a chartered accountant.

He was an intelligent man, so his success surprised no one. He even applied to the *Institute of Chartered Accountants of Nigeria (ICAN)* and was certified by the organization.

The newly-married couple were not rich, despite Simbiat's wealthy background, but they believed that things would take a turn for the better. Simbiat was instrumental in MKO's financial success some years later. They spent a total of six years in Glasgow before returning to their home country. It was enough time to make a name for themselves, earn valuable experience, and even have some children! Once back in Nigeria, Simbi got a job as an Arts Lecturer at the *Yaba College of Technology* since she already had experience teaching in Scotland. Her classes taught the Art of Tie-Dye. MKO, likewise, had no difficulty finding employment. *The University of Lagos Teaching Hospital* — now known as *LUTH* — took him on to become one of their senior accountants.

Chapter IV — Thinking Big

Pfizer Failure and ITT Corp

MKO stayed at LUTH for only a short while because he soon began working for Pfizer, the pharmaceutical giant.
Abiola was a dreamer... and he dreamt big!
He knew that owning a percentage of Pfizer would serve him far better than a simple salary. So he approached his boss. "I'd like to speak to you about part-ownership in Pfizer," he said. His boss listened intently, but unfortunately, Pfizer's terms were not satisfying — to say the very least — so Abiola switched his focus to something more promising.
He found a job listing for a company that needed to hire a trained accountant. The name of the company was not listed but he applied anyway. At the job interview, he learned that he had applied to a company called International Telephone and Telegraph. The firm's management quickly recognized his brilliant mind and he was hired right away.

Meeting with the Nigerian Military

Little did he know how difficult his first task on the job would be! His boss tasked him with convincing the Nigerian military to pay back all it owed to ITT Corp. This seemingly-impossible task did not deter the ambitious man. He began to work immediately.

He called the office of the Inspector of Signals of the Nigerian Army and set up a meeting to meet with man in charge, Murtala Muhammed.

The meeting did not go as planned.

When it began, Abiola presented his case to Murtala Muhammed, explaining why ITT Corp should get its money back. A loud argument could be heard down the halls and all throughout the building. It even got the attention of the Chief of Army Staff, who burst into the room, and demanded to know what the commotion was all about.

MKO explained to the Chief that ITT Corp was owed a large sum of money and needed to collect. Inspector Muhammed was shocked when the Chief immediately ordered a cheque be written and the debt fully paid.

Abiola had convinced him it was the right thing to do. "Please write this man a cheque, Inspector. The full amount."

"Chief," Inspector Muhammed objected. "Are you sure we should be—"

"Am I sure of what, Inspector?" The Chief interrupted, fully in command. "Am I sure that the Nigerian Army pays its debts? Yes, you bet I am."

The Inspector fell silent. He had overstepped his bounds. MKO left the building soon after.

The cheque was proof of his success.

If he were able to continue showing his superiors this sort of success, then one day, he could ask for part-ownership in ITT Corp! He wanted to own 50% of ITT's Nigerian branch of the company.

He did eventually approach the company with his proposal. Unfortunately, they turned him down. Abiola was disappointed in the outcome but did manage to have the foreign manager of the company removed.

It was a minor victory.

Business Mogul

Abiola realized that if he could not get partial ownership in ITT Corp, he could always start his own company. He established Radio Communication Nigeria (RCN), a communications company that hired and trained employees to market telecommunications equipment. The meeting with the Nigerian Army had sparked an idea within the man: His company could sell directly to the military! MKO had learned that the army was in the process of upgrading their civil-war-era equipment; a perfect opportunity for business. He made a plan they could not refuse! "RCN will train your personnel to use and maintain the equipment," he proposed to the Nigerian Army. "That way, you won't ever have to depend on outside contractors for help." The military loved the idea. Security was of utmost concern to the Nigerian military leaders.
This proposal would solve all their worries in one shot! Since they did not want to look too eager — which would have surrendered all their bargaining power — they told him they would think about it and get back to him.
RCN got the contract. The business deal impressed and worried ITT Corp. Their relevance in dealing with the army was at stake! They knew they had to partner with Abiola if they were to successfully remain in the market. So, they offered him 49% ownership in the Nigerian subsidiary of ITT Corp. It was not 50% but Abiola took what he could get! This propelled him into the business world.

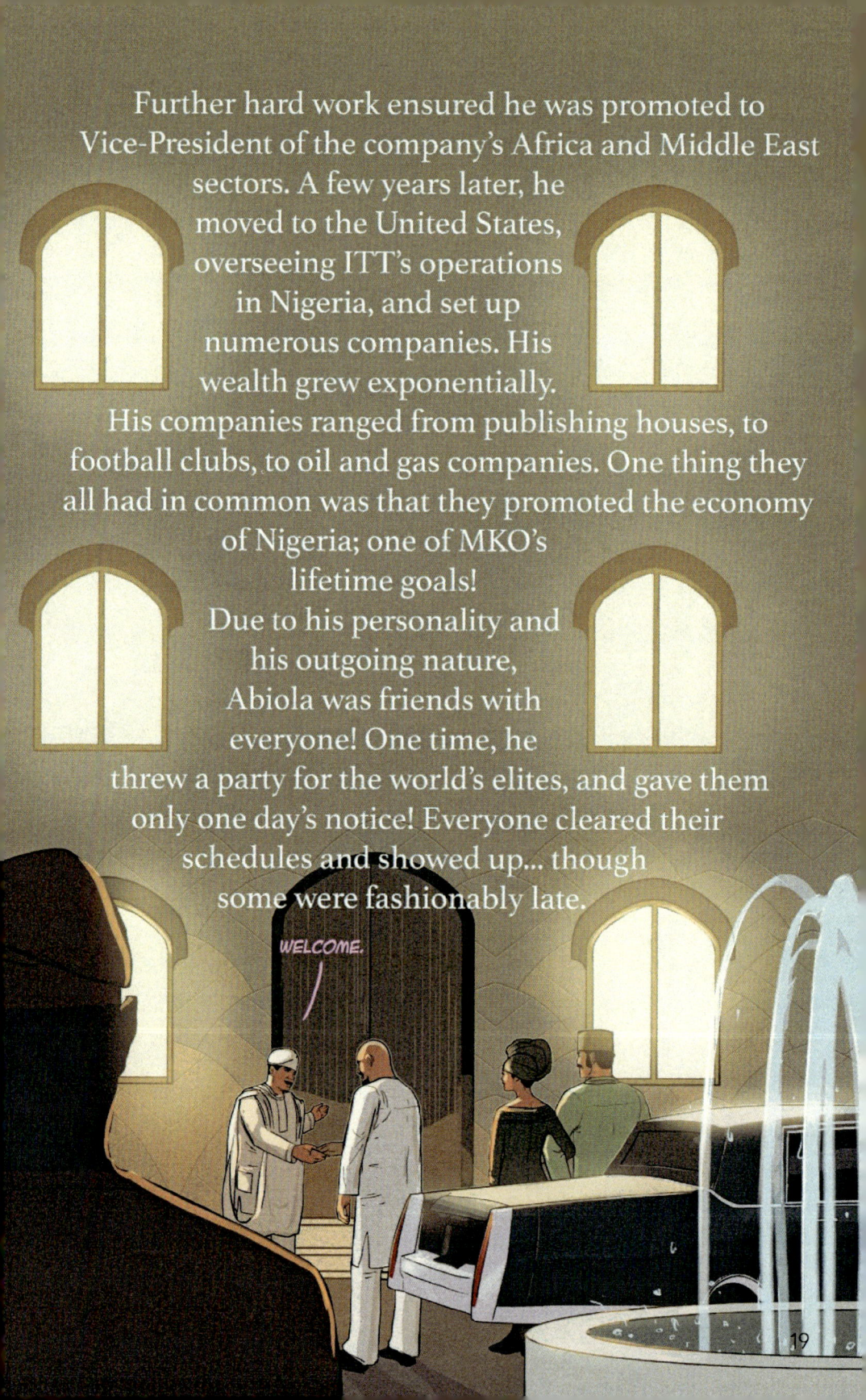

Further hard work ensured he was promoted to Vice-President of the company's Africa and Middle East sectors. A few years later, he moved to the United States, overseeing ITT's operations in Nigeria, and set up numerous companies. His wealth grew exponentially.

His companies ranged from publishing houses, to football clubs, to oil and gas companies. One thing they all had in common was that they promoted the economy of Nigeria; one of MKO's lifetime goals!

Due to his personality and his outgoing nature, Abiola was friends with everyone! One time, he threw a party for the world's elites, and gave them only one day's notice! Everyone cleared their schedules and showed up... though some were fashionably late.

WELCOME.

But Abiola did not discriminate; he loved the regular people and they loved him back! He invested heavily in the lower classes by donating to charities and for scholarships. Abiola even fought to restore Africa's lost integrity! He actively sent petitions to the United States and certain European countries, asking for compensation for Africa for the many decades of colonialism and African enslavement. His political beliefs were already evident, long before he became a politician. MKO's business sense is celebrated to this day. He is considered one of Nigeria's most successful businessmen of all time. He even managed to become the President of the Nigerian Stock Exchange; not bad, right?!

Among his most famous companies are Abiola Farms, Abiola Bookshops, Abiola Football Club, RCN, Concord Press, Concord Airlines, Wonder Bakeries, Summit Oil International Ltd., and Habib Bank.

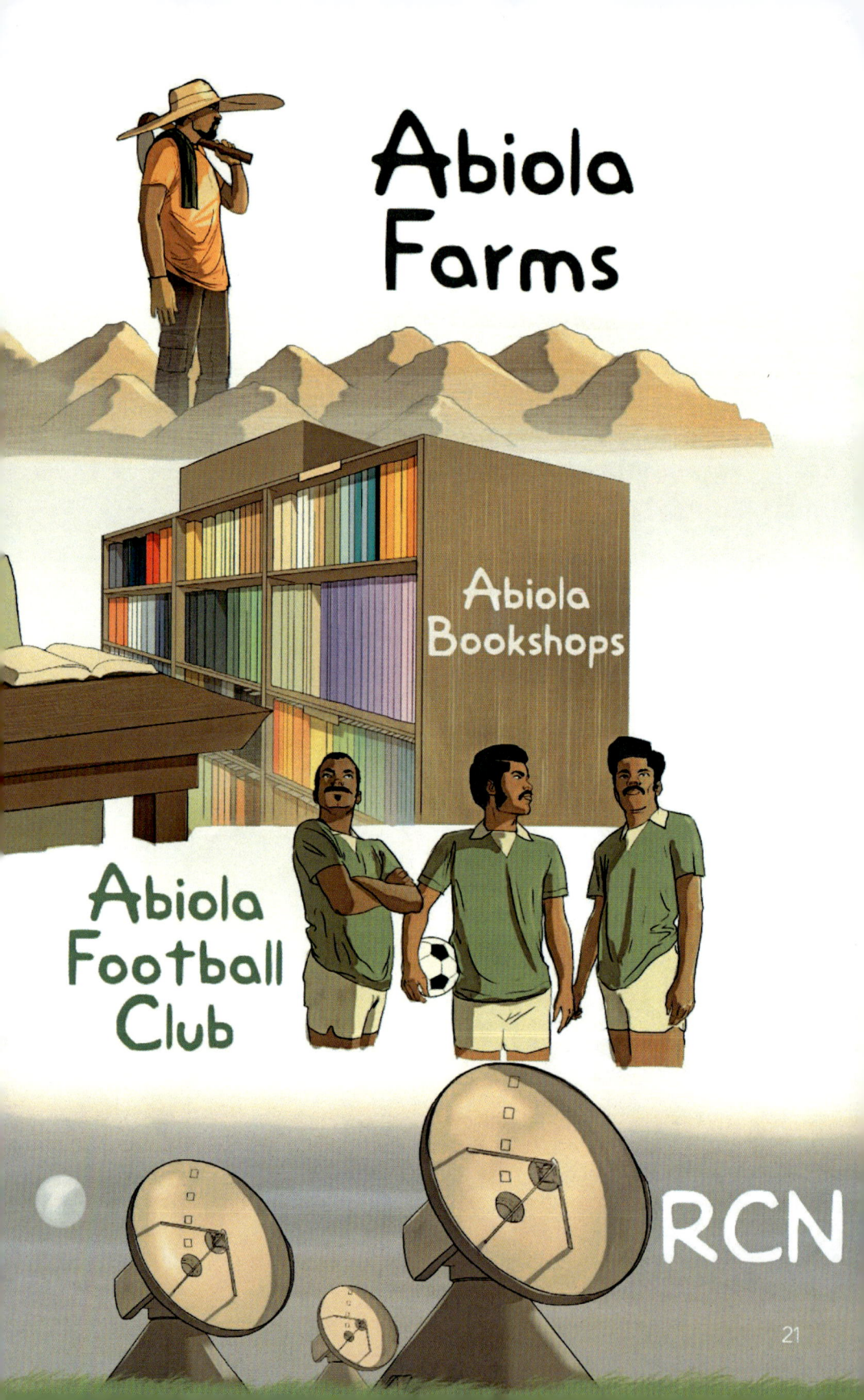

Abiola Farms

Abiola Bookshops

Abiola Football Club

RCN

21

Concord Press

Concord Airlines

Wonder Bakeries

Summit Oil International Ltd.

Habib Bank

Chapter V — Politics

State Chairman of NPN

In 1979, the Nigerian government was controlled by a brutal military regime.
Abiola had joined the National Party of Nigeria (NPN), which was the ruling party, in hopes of steering Nigeria in the proper direction; away from military rule.
While he had been politically interested since the age of 19 when he had first joined the NCNC, the situation in Nigeria had grown so desperate, Abiola felt he had no choice but to join the political fight. Within a short amount of time, Abiola was elected the NPN's State Chairman, and things were looking up. The NPN had just won another election!
MKO was now eligible to run for Nigerian President! From that position, he could do immense work and help the Nigerian people in a meaningful way.

Coup D'Etat and Death of a Loved One

Unfortunately, things took a turn for the worse when the country's military staged another coup d'etat and eliminated civilian rule for 10 years!

It was a terrible decade for the citizens of Nigeria. Misery was felt at all levels of society, from the poor to the rich. The military regime created many anti-civilian policies to ensure the army's hard-handed control.

With not much left to lose, the people of Nigeria began to demand change! They were tired of oppression! All classes of society were speaking in unison and the military government could no longer pretend not to hear!

Under intense social pressure, General Ibrahim Babangida, the Head of State at the time, relented and returned civilian control to the country. Democracy had returned to Nigeria.

The celebrations at the Abiola household were cut short when his wife, Simbiat, fell ill.

She was flown to London where she received treatment. Tragically, it was not enough to save her and she died on November 10th, 1992.

General Ibrahim Babangida attended her funeral, as did other high-profile members of society. He even spoke at the funeral and told Abiola something which would stick with the new widower all his life.

People's Man, People's President

"You should run for President, Abiola.", the General said to hushed gasps in the room; it was very unexpected coming from him. He continued, "Nigeria is ready to have you as President, all you need to do is run the campaign."

The shocking revelation by General Babangida made sense. Many of MKO's businesses were centered around helping the masses. His Abiola bookshops provided locally-produced textbooks, since foreign textbooks were expensive and difficult to find. His Abiola farms provided basic daily necessities — like rice and soap — at affordable prices. The people already loved him. He had simply not noticed how much. MKO brushed off the compliment with a polite laugh, but that night, he began to think about the possibilities. Maybe, just maybe, the people of Nigeria wanted him to be their next president.

Chapter VI — The Presidential Election

The Political Journey

In the early stages, Abiola's presidential aspirations were met with some resistance.

During the primary elections in the new Social Democratic Party (SDP), Abiola was up against two opponents, Ambassador Kingibe and Atiku Abubakar.

Not everyone in the SDP was happy with his desire to run. "You are simply too young, Abiola," one member of the party told him. "You are too inexperienced. Leave it to those who have been here longer."

The successful businessman agreed with the sentiment... mostly. "That's precisely the problem," MKO replied. "I believe that Nigeria is ready for something new."

The man stood up, offended by the implication. "You don't know what you're talking about, Abiola," he said; his anger was evident. "You'll ruin this country!"

The party's primaries came down to a vote for MKO or Ambassador Kingibe. In the first round, Abiola won by majority over Kingibe who was right behind him. The Ambassador was not about to give up and contested the election. When the second primary round was held, Abiola came out victorious again. It was undeniable. He was the party's preferred presidential candidate!

Thank you.

The Campaign

Abiola had no time to waste. The June 12th election was fast approaching so he had to campaign right away!
He ran on several slogans, each of which promised a better future for Nigerians of all classes. The campaign ran ads promising "Farewell to Poverty," the "Burden of Schooling," and the popular "At last! Our Ray of Hope!"

The economic situation in the country was especially important to the people. They were struggling. They had no money to pay for necessities and little hope for change. "My children's school needs better supplies," MKO heard a desperate Nigerian woman yell at one of his rallies. Others were calling for cheaper food prices.
Abiola promised the people that he would re-negotiate Nigeria's debts to international banks; with a better deal, their economic burden would lessen. He also promised that he would manage the debts much better than his predecessors.
It was hard not to believe him. Abiola was widely respected in international circles. He had dealt with many investors through his business dealings. If anyone was to be trusted with Nigeria's economy, it was him.

The Election

By January 5th, 1993, over 250 candidates had been screened by the National Electoral Commission (NEC), which oversaw the election. Many of the candidates and parties were disqualified for one reason or another. Abiola cleared the commission and was grated permission to run. Ambassador Kingibe, not one to be left out of the spotlight, became Abiola's running mate. If elected, he would be Nigeria's next Vice-President; not a bad position to be in on his way to the top. "Abiola," the Ambassador nodded to his running mate as they stepped on stage for their final rally. Both men were savvy-enough politically to know that they only stood to gain from cooperation. "Kingibe," Abiola returned the greeting as the two candidates waved to the adoring crowd. The election was held on June 12th, a day with extremely bad weather.

It was so bad, the candidates believed that many citizens would stay home instead of voting, but they were wrong! Over 14 million Nigerians braved the bad weather to exercise their right to vote! Their choices were clear: Choose MKO and the Social Democratic Party, or choose Bashir Tofa and the National Republican Convention. Everyone eagerly awaited the results.

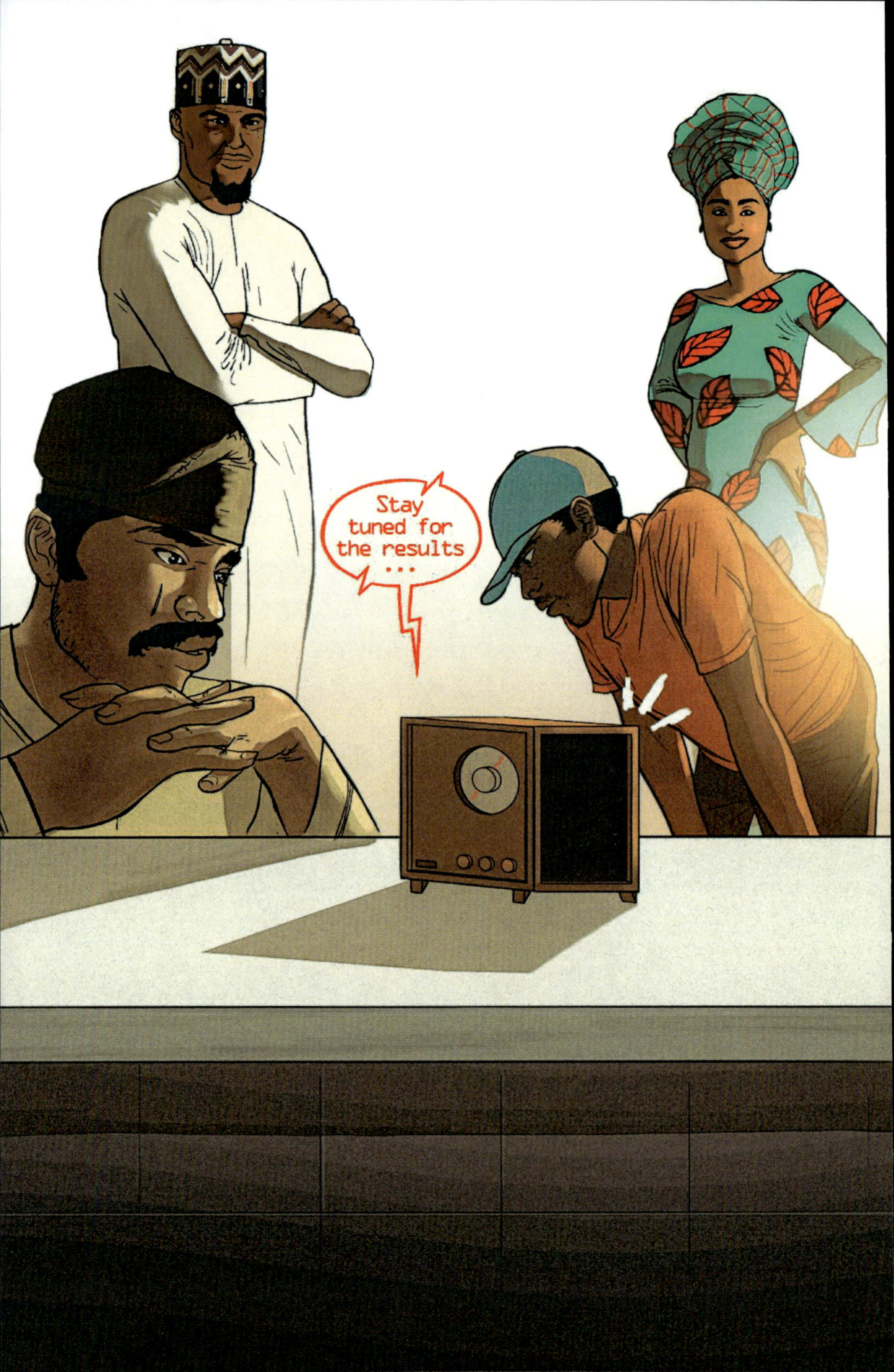
Stay tuned for the results ...

Chapter VII — The Annulment

The Results?

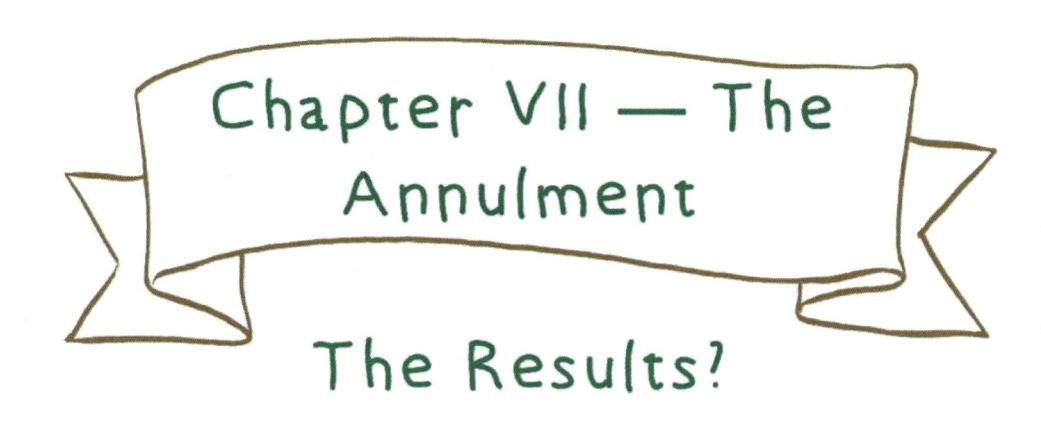

Their excitement did not last very long because the results of the June 12 presidential election were never released. Certain civil society groups gathered polling data and compiled it. It revealed that the Social Democratic Party was greatly favored in the election. It also indicated that the people had chosen Chief Moshood Kashimawo Olawale Abiola as their new president!

But, General Ibrahim Babangida had decided the election should be annulled. As the current Head of State, it was something he could do; not to mention that he had the Nigerian military at his fingertips!

When pressed on why, the General claimed that he was trying to save the nation from harm and said that suspicious political activities took place during the election.
General Babangida did not elaborate further when pressed for specifics. His declaration baffled Nigerians at home and abroad! Many people had been pleasantly surprised by the peaceful nature of the election — much different than it had been in the past — there were so many concerns. Others even believed that these had been the fairest and freest presidential elections in Nigeria's history!
Despite the court siding with the General, a group called Campaign for Democracy illegally released the results from the polling booths. It clearly showed that Abiola had won by majority of the votes!
He had received an estimated 8.34 million votes while Tofa had gotten 5.95 million.

The Interim Government

Internationally, the United States and Great Britain took away aid from the country in protest of the election's annulment. This was meant to put pressure on the government to relent, but all it did was cause suffering for the Nigerian people. General Babangida, on the other hand, had no intention of changing his mind.
The uncertainty and the deteriorating economic situation reignited Nigerian demands for political change!

Then, shortly after announcing he would step down on August 26th, 1993, General Babangida created the *Interim National Government (ING)* to run Nigeria. At first, it was first run by a man named Ernest Shonekan, but he ruled Nigeria very briefly, about three months! His tenure started on August 27th and ended on November 17th, 1993, when General Sani Abacha staged a bloodless coup on the Presidential Palace.

Sani Abacha's Reign

Bloodless coup or not, General Sani Abacha's actions ushered in another decade of autocratic rule in Nigeria.

It would take a big stretch of the imagination to call his rule benevolent! His opponents accused him of using very heavy-handed tactics. Abiola, who at the time was out of the country, rallied for international support in opposition to the General. Meanwhile, large protests and massive civil unrest rocked Nigeria, especially in the south-west of the country. MKO travelled to London — where he stayed for several months — to speak out about the situation in his country. He had access to many influential people and it would have been a waste not to seek their help. On the 1st anniversary of the annulled election, Abiola gave a very famous speech, where he declared himself the democratically elected President of Nigeria. "I call on the military leaders to step down and return civilian rule to Nigeria…", Abiola's voice spoke from a television set in General Sani Abacha's office. "As President, I am forming a new government and reinstating the House of Representatives."

The General turned the TV off with his remote and picked up a phone.
"Yes, sir?" Asked a voice on the line.
"Send some men to arrest, Abiola."
"General?"
"I believe I've made myself very clear!"
Sani Abacha said in a cold voice.
"Right away, General," the man apologized.
General Abacha hung up the phone, lit a cigar, and sat back in his chair. He had hoped to use his power as military president to forcefully become the democratically elected president. There was no way he would let Abiola ruin that!

Chapter VIII — Legacy of an Icon

Prison

Prison was not kind to MKO. He spent a total of four years imprisoned under General Sani Abacha's reign in power. There were speculations that MKO was beaten and maltreated while in custody, though there are no official admissions to the claims unfortunately. However, the time he spent in prison was an unfortunate one for him, his family and avid supporters. No one believed he deserved to be in prison. He deserved so much more having lived a truly fulfilling and impactful life.

Two years after his imprisonment, his senior wife, Kudirat, who had been campaigning for his release, was assassinated by gunmen in the capital city; Lagos, Nigeria.

Kudirat was shot by assassins while she was in her car in the capital city. Her death was a huge loss to the entire family and MKO Abiola supporters in Nigeria as a whole. The family and supporters mourned deeply and continually sort for justice to be done. It was indeed a sad day and series of events in the memory of the family, well wishers and supporters.

The loss of his senior wife was also a very sad one for the inspiring man - MKO Abiola, but there was even more to come two years later, a loss that will change the cause of history and the story of the iconic legend forever.

Death of a Legend

One day, Abiola was visited in prison by a delegation from the United States. The visitors were top government officials! The former US Ambassador to Nigeria, Thomas Pickering, was in attendance, as were: Bill Twadell (the current-at-the-time Ambassador), and Susan Rice, the Assistant Secretary.

"It's a pleasure to meet you," Ambassador Twadell said extending his hand. Abiola shook it, giving his own pleasantries. "Likewise, Ambassador."

They sat down and began the visit, but before long, to ask him if he was okay, but before she could, MKO collapsed in his seat.

The delegation called for help, which soon arrived. Several men took Abiola to the hospital, but later, the official statement said he was already dead by the time he got there. The cause of death listed on the autopsy was a massive heart attack. It was July 7th, 1998.

Lasting Legacy

Abiola's death was very painful and sad for the majority of the Nigerian people.

Subsequent governments tried but failed to recognize the politician, even under great pressure from the citizens. For years and years, activist groups lobbied to have the traditional annual Democracy Day celebrations switched from May 29th to June 12th, to commemorate the late MKO Abiola.

Politicians in power had no intention of validating his 1993 victory at the polls. It would have been a major embarrassment for many officials if they had shown him such national honor.

But the pressure mounted and in 2018, the Nigerian government of President Muhammadu Buhari posthumously conferred upon Abiola the highest Nigerian honor – (GCFR) Grand Commander of the Federal Republic.

Today, Nigeria's Democracy Day is celebrated on June 12th in honor of Moshood Kashimawo Olawale Abiola, the People's President.

MKO Abiola's iconic legacy and impact lives on in his children around the world, with his family, with his avid supporters, in the lives of many Nigerians (young and old) and in growing generations who are constantly paving the way in different strides and achievements positively across the world.

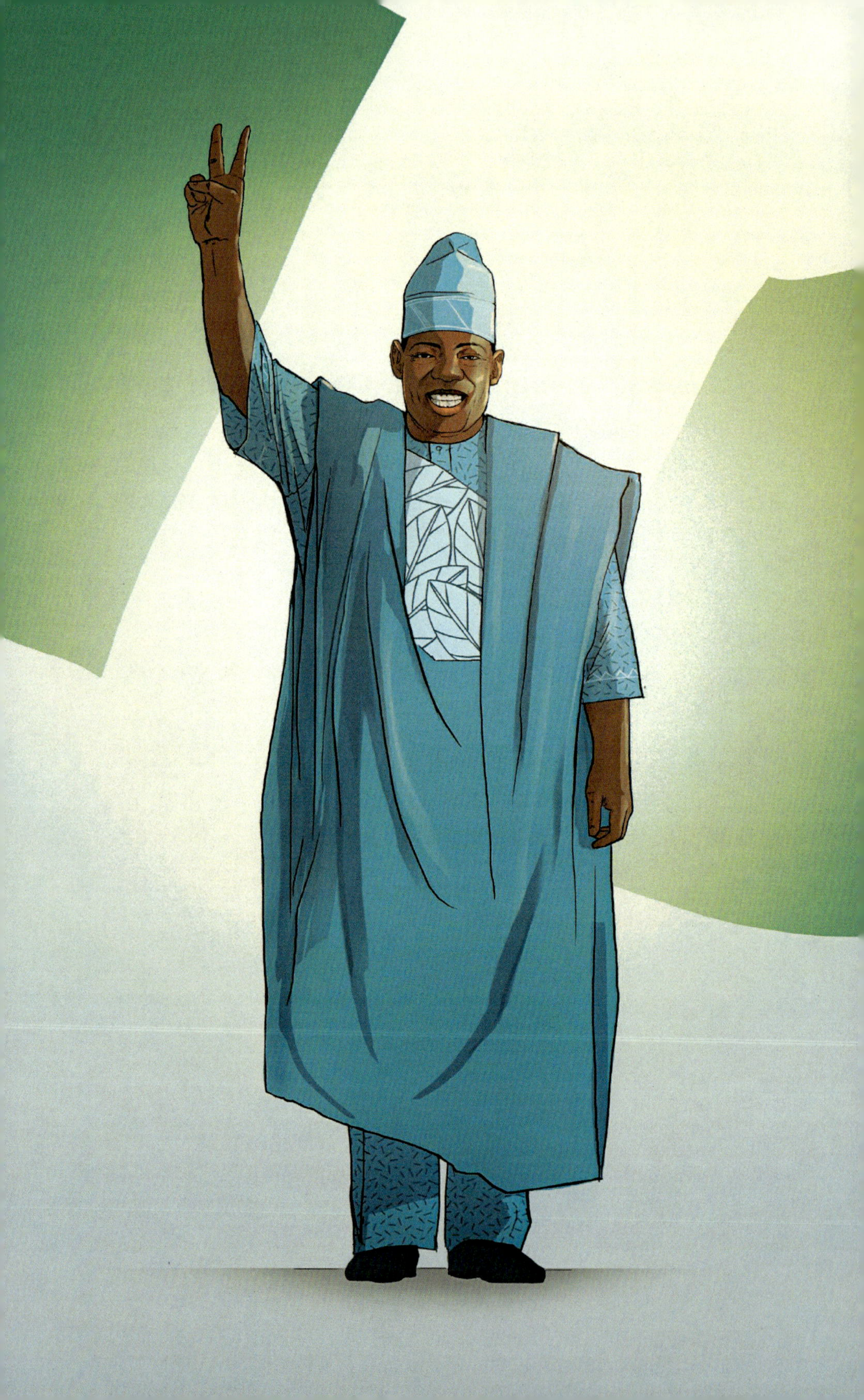

TIMELINE FOR MKO ABIOLA'S LIFE

1937 - Born in Ogun state to a family of modest income

1960 - Wins a scholarship to study Accounting at Glasgow university

1970 - Begins to ride Nigeria's oil boom to wealth;

1979 - Nigerian military government hands over government to civilians, MKO Abiola joins a party and Shehu Shagari wins elections

1983 - December Gen Muhammadu Buhari comes to power in a military regime

1985 - Gen Buhari is deposed and Gen Babangida takes over.

1990 - MKO concentrates on his airline and shipping business

1993 - Abiola runs on SDP ticket and wins election by voting results.

1993 - Abacha assumes absolute Power

1994 - MKO is arrested for declaring himself as president.

1996 - MKO Abiola's senior wife, Kudirat, is assassinated by gunmen after campaigning for his release

1998 (July) Moshood Kashimawo Olawale Abiola is pronounced dead on the 7th of July

—

Posthumous Honour

2018 (June 6th) - Awarded the Highest Nigerian Honour - GCFR posthumously by the Nigerian Democratic President Muhammadu Buhari.

ACCLAIMED FAMOUS SAYINGS BY MKO ABIOLA

- No one can give you power. It is yours. Take it! From this day, show to the world that anyone who takes the people of Nigeria for fools is deceiving himself and will have the people to answer to.

- If you want something from a dwarf, stoop low to his level. It does not reduce your own height. Whenever you rise up, you will be taller than him.

- Only real democracy can move our nation forward towards progress, and earn her the respect she deserves from the international community.

- A scarcity of books and equipment has rendered our schools into desolate deserts of ignorance

- You cannot shave the head in the absence of the owner.

- Those with whom I have sought to dialogue have remained like stones, neither stirred to show loyalty to the collective decision of the people of their own country, nor to observe.

- If you go borrowing, you will go a-sorrowing

- Enough of square pegs in round holes... Enough is enough

GLOSSARY

Abeokuta - A city in Nigeria, West Africa.

Ambassador - A person sent by a country to another country as a representative.

Ambitious - Go after something hard to get

Aspirations - Dreams or hopes for the future

Autopsy - A medical test used to know the cause of death.

Awkward - Feeling uneasy or embarrassed

Beat all odds - To succeed even despite lack of support unhelpful situations

Beneath - Under

Bloodless coup - A take over of the government with no death or blood spilled.

Blossomed - Grew

Brutal - Wicked

Charities - Organizations that help others

Chief Obafemi Awolowo - first Premier of the Western Region in Nigeria, a nationalist, and a principal participant in the struggle for Nigeria's independence.

Chipper- Happy

Collapsed- Fell down

Colonialism- The act of a country controlling another country

Commotion- Noise causing event

Compliment - Kind words to describe a person or something.

Control- Gives orders and instructions

Coup D'état - removal of the government of a country by force

Dawn – The first hour of daylight

Decade - Ten years

Delegation - A set of people chosen to represent a larger group.

Deserved - Gotten because of something done well

Desperate- In great need.

Destined - Meant to

Destroyed - To break something down to ruins

Deteriorating - Going bad

Difficult - Not easy

Disapproved- To not support a decision because you believe it wrong.

Discourage - To lose hope.

Discriminate- To see one as lesser than the other.

Disease - A terrible sickness

Donating- To give freely to help someone else.

Eligible - Have the ability to be chosen

Eliminated - To be removed

Enslavement- To make people slaves.

Ensured- To make sure

Exponentially- Increasingly

Exported- To send out goods or services to another country.

Extended - Increased in length, width, years

Flagged- Stopped.

Folklore - Stories about the cultural origin of a group of people.

Genuine - Real

Glasgow - A city in Scotland

Haggis - A dish from Scotland.

Hard-handed - To be too harsh

Heavy-handed - To use too much force

High-achievers - People who work hard to achieve their goals

High-risk/high-reward - The possibility of getting either a major loss or major profit.

Immense - Very large

Implication - The result of an action

Inexperienced - To have no previous knowledge of a thing

Integrity- Honesty

Kerosene - A liquid used as a fuel for light, heat or power.

Legacy - Causing a big impact on people

Massive - very big

Meaningful - Gives meaning and importance

Minor - Small

Mogul - important person of power

Numerous - Plenty

Oppression - Wicked show of power over others

Outcome - What happens after an action.

Oversaw - To observe all that went on

Overstep - To go past where one is allowed.

Permission - Act of allowing something

Petitions - Formal written document

Pleased - To be satisfied.

Posthumously - After the person's death.

Precisely - Exactly

Preferred - Chose one over another

Presidential Palace - official home of the president

Prominent - Popular

Propelled - Push forward

Reignited - To start again

Relented - Reduced

Reserved - Set aside

Resistance - To act against

Risk - To be exposed to danger, harm or loss

Routine - A repeated activity

Savvy-enough - To know a subject well enough.

Scandalous - Something that causes a person's reputation (how he is known) to go bad/wrong.

Scotland - A country that is part of the United Kingdom

Sensational - very interesting

Sentiment - General feeling

Shipment - Goods shipped

Staged - Planned/prepared

Steering - Leading

Studious - People who are committed to their academics or work

Survive - To continue to live

Telegraph - Tool for sending written information over a distance

Terrible - Very bad

Thrilled - To feel happy

Tradesman - A person into buying and selling.

Tragically - Sadly

Turn down - To reject

Unfortunately - Sadly

Uttering - Saying

Valuable - Worth the effort

Witness - To see

Yoruba – A major ethnic language spoken in nigeria

BIBLIOGRAPHY

Here are some of the references we had fun working with to create this amazing book:

Britannica, T. Editors of Encyclopedia. <u>Moshood Kashimawo Olawale Abiola.</u> 2022.

Fayemiwo, Moshood. M.K.O Abiola: <u>The Authorized Biography Of Chief Moshood Kasimawo Olawale Abiola Winner Of June 12, 1993 Presidential Election In Nigeria.</u> US-African Christian Publishing Incorporated, 2003.

Ogunlana, Femi. <u>The life, speech & death of MKO: A manual that drums the basic lessons of leadership to Nigerians.</u> Glazocum Media Co., Ogbomoso, 1998.

Omoniyi, Tosin; Adenekan, Samson. <u>Democracy Day: MKO Abiola in the eyes of history 27 years later.</u> 2020.

Opara, Bartholomew. <u>June 12, 1993 Presidential Election.</u> Subavic International, 2007.

Oyibode, Austin. <u>The inside story of the brutal murder of Kudirat Abiola in Lagos in 1996.</u> 2017.

Sahara reporters. <u>JUNE 12 SPECIAL: Short Profile of Late Chief MKO Abiola.</u> New York, 2021.

Sodimu, Sunday A. <u>Abiola, the Man of the People: His Life, Political Ambition, Incarceration, and Death.</u> Miral Printing Press, Lagos, 1998.

ABOUT THE 'BIG' SERIES

BE INSPIRED BY THE GREATEST SERIES

The vision of The "BIG" Series – "Be Inspired by the Greatest" is to retell the stories of African Inspiring People beyond the boundaries of the African continent to children across the world.

Internationally, Inspire HQ writes these stories to connect our young readers to the lives of these African inspiring characters, with a vision to inspire our readers to see beyond the character, to learn from them and recreate the experiences of their lives.

At Inspire HQ, we hope every book inspires the reader to do more, be more and shine on.
Be Inspired On!

For information: www.myinspirebooks.com

Inspire HQ

ABOUT THE AUTHOR

Olamidotun is a successful entrepreneur, a children's book author, and a prolific speaker. As a child, she read several books about great people, and this motivated her to be more than she ever dreamt of. Her daughter's love for stories about historic people inspired her journey into writing. She writes to inspire her three daughters and every child around the world to dream and be all they can be to change the world around them positively.

In 2019, an international business publication named Olamidotun on the list of 100 most inspiring women in celebration of International Women's Day.

Find out more about the author here:
www.olamidotunvo.com

Manufactured by Amazon.ca
Acheson, AB